How to Create a Meaningful Future

15 Empowering Steps to Reach Your Summit

Rená Koesler has an insatiable drive to help others unearth their potential. She has inspired many. She specifically uses her life experiences of climbing mountains to teach others the power in hard work, determination, overcoming adversity and living a goal oriented, zestful life.

In her first Itty Bitty Book, Koesler gives you the 15 Empowering Steps to Reach Each Summit – the metaphor she uses in her workshops and keynote addresses to challenge her audiences to *MOVE*.

- Make your life count: Go for what you want.

- Get up, stand up, and move towards your goal.

- Don't stop at one success; keep on chasing.

If you have a goal or dream you want to achieve, this book will get you there. Order this Itty Bitty Book today and start your journey.

Your Amazing Itty Bitty® Achieving Your Potential

15 Empowering Steps to Reach Each Summit

Rená A. Koesler

Published by Itty Bitty® Publishing
A subsidiary of S & P Productions, Inc.

Copyright © 2020 Rená A. Koesler

All rights reserved. No part of this book may be reproduced or transmitted in any form or by any means, electronic or mechanical, including photocopying, recording or by any information storage and retrieval system, without written permission of the publisher, except for inclusion of brief quotations in a review.

Printed in the United States of America

Itty Bitty Publishing
311 Main Street, Suite D
El Segundo, CA 90245
(310) 640-8885

ISBN: 978-1-950326-58-7

I am thankful to those friends and family members who encouraged me to "write a book." To my initial meeting with Suzy Prudden and beyond; Thank you for your belief in my idea and your support and encouragement along the way. This Itty Bitty Book project has sparked my enthusiasm to continue writing and sharing in the future.

Stop by our Itty Bitty® website Directory to find interesting goal setting and coaching information.

www.IttyBittyPublishing.com

Or visit Rená A. Koesler
at: www.renakoesler.com

Table of Contents

Step 1.	Identify Your Summit
Step 2.	Your WHY
Step 3.	Vision to Reality
Step 4.	Plan Ahead
Step 5.	Do Your Homework
Step 6.	It's Okay to Ask for Help
Step 7.	Choose Your Thoughts
Step 8.	Step into the Arena
Step 9.	Faith in the Midst
Step 10.	Put One Foot in Front of the Other
Step 11.	Pull Out Your Compass
Step 12.	Keep the Momentum
Step 13.	Celebrate Your Summit
Step 14.	Power of Reflection
Step 15.	Seek Your Next Summit

Introduction

Growing up in the Midwest I had no thought about climbing a mountain let alone reaching a summit of any kind. I don't think I had sights on achieving anything out of the ordinary. I bumbled along like every other 21-year old in my social circle, doing what they did and being what I thought I was supposed to be-UNTIL I climbed my first mountain on October 1, 1977. It was hard work and far beyond my comfort zone. But, through the challenge, I unearthed my internal will and desire.

When I reached the top and returned to the base of the mountain I wanted to repeat that experience over and over again. I couldn't wait to take this new inspiration and pass it on to others. I have chased much more than mountain summits ever since.

This book is meant as an essential guide to reach your potential. Believe in your vision that WILL get you to your goal. Stop bumbling around, stop making excuses, put one foot in front of the other, and step out into the unknown. Your summit is achievable. You will get to the top, and the views will be amazing!

Step 1
Identify Your Summit

It's a round trip. Getting to the summit is optional, getting down is mandatory.
~ Ed Viesturs

A summit is a goal, a dream, a desire or something you wish to pursue, but haven't started yet or are stuck in the process.

There are those who can identify their summit, but often need guidance to begin their move toward it. Some summits are identified completely by surprise, as mine was. Others have difficulty finding their summit(s) or know how to ignite their goals or dreams.

1. Identify a summit that YOU want to pursue, not what others want for you.
2. Take the time necessary to explore your interests and prospective goals.
3. Talk to others who you know and trust. Invite them to help you narrow down your potential summit(s).
4. Explore your interests and talents in a way that will illuminate your desire and internal compass.

Establish Your Summit

- What are your strengths? Talents? Gifts?
- What are you good at accomplishing?
- What do you enjoy doing?
- Have you ever said "I wish I could do that!?"
- What comes natural or easy for you?
- Is there a role model or mentor who exhibits a behavior or action that you admire?
- What mental bells ring or emotional sparks arise when you engage in a particular behavior or experience?
- Record the answers to the above questions and discern a theme that emerges when you review your answers side by side.

Step 2
Your WHY

The two most important days of your life are the day you were born and the day you discovered why.
~ Mark Twain

Knowing your WHY or your purpose for reaching your potential is the most vital step in your summiting process. There is longevity in your success when you authentically believe in your summit pursuit. As Abraham Lincoln said, "nothing will divert me from my purpose." Align your values, passions and strengths with your WHY.

1. Take time and respect the process of identifying your WHY.
2. Invest in the time and depth of thought. It will clear the way for the rest of the steps to naturally fall into place.
3. Be careful of identifying money or fame as your WHY. Money or fame is often the result of achieving your WHY.
4. Believe in yourself. No one ever outperforms their own self-image.
5. Believe in your WHY. Belief drives behavior.

WHY your WHY?

The following questions will determine whether you are on the right path toward your summit. Having solid answers to these questions will ensure that meaning and value are associated with your WHY.

- How will your WHY benefit you?
- How will your WHY benefit others?
- Will your WHY inspire you or others to go beyond your perceived abilities?
- Does your WHY give you freedom and motivation to explore and reach your potential?
- Does your WHY breathe confidence and enthusiasm when asked by others?

    **The Strength of your WHY will give momentum to "what" you do and "how" you will do it.

Step 3
Vision to Reality

Imagination is everything. It is a preview of life's coming attractions.
~ Albert Einstein

Your vision fast forwards a mental picture and anticipates what you imagine seeing and feeling when you reach your goal or summit.

1. The emotions stirred from your vision will motivate you to ACTION with focus and determination.
2. Your vision provides momentum, allowing you to move upward and onward.
3. Your vision should align with your WHY because your WHY keeps your vision in view.
4. Ensure your vision is worth pursuing so that there is no chance of abandoning it.
5. Don't expect others to be excited about your vision. Your vision is all yours.

Is this YOUR Vision?

- Does your vision ignite a sense of vitality and awareness in you?
- Is your vision challenging enough to extend beyond your comfort zone?
- Are you willing to fulfill the vision that you imagine?
- What views do you see when you reach your summit?
- What roles do your friends and family play in your vision?
- Are you ready to commit to your vision?
- How fulfilled will you be once your vision becomes reality?
- Know your vision is YOURS and not a vision passed on to you from someone else.

Step 4
Plan Ahead

*Tell me, what is it you plan to do with
your one wild and precious life?*
~ Mary Oliver

You need to have a plan to grow and be better today than you were yesterday. Planning for an upcoming trip, an event or even a Thanksgiving meal requires an organized sequence of details. These details provide the trail map for how your plan will unfold over your determined time to reach your goal.

1. Create a calendar that includes specific actions plans. Write it out and place it in clear view as a visual reminder.
2. Differentiate among the tasks by highlighting them in various colors.
3. Be consistent in your plan. This will eventually form a habit and more easily become part of your daily routine.
4. Stay focused on your plan. Reduce or eliminate the "squirrels" (distractions) that surround you.

Time and Time Again

You can't manage your time since the amount of time is the same from day to day. But, you can manage your priorities.

- Get up in the morning, carve out your day and set your plan in motion.
- Hold yourself accountable and respect your plan. More than anyone, you don't want to disappoint yourself.
- Stick to your plan, as long as it is serving you and your direction. If not, alter your plan.
- Your vision will give your plan the strength necessary to commit to seeing it through.

Do not underestimate the power of commitment. The greater the commitment to your plan, the greater the belief in reaching your goal.

- Create a contract with yourself to follow through.
- Make your plan a priority.

Step 5
Do Your Homework

It's not the will to win that matters... It's the will to prepare to win that matters.
~ Paul "Bear" Bryant

Preparation follows your plan. Without a plan in place, you don't know what kind, or amount of preparation is involved. When you prepare for a meal you are serving, you pull together the ingredients, light the oven, set the timer and get ready for cooking. The same is true for pursuing your potential. You have to set the table before a meal can be served.

1. If you need to study, study.
2. If you need to learn something, learn it AND learn from the right people.
3. If you need special skills, get trained on those special skills.
4. If you need more experience, get the experience necessary from those you trust.
5. If you need to understand, seek understanding.

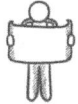

Make Your Homework Count

Eliminate the phrases "I can't" or "I don't know how."

- If you need to connect with others, be intentional about making that connection.
- If you want to improve, strive to make improvements every day.
- If you want to overcome, fight; really fight to overcome.
- Seek to understand as this is the gateway to doing and being your best.

Believe you can DO more and BE more than your perceptions allow. Spend time with others who inspire you and want to see you grow.

Step 6
It's Okay to Ask for Help

Mentoring is a brain to pick, an ear to listen and a push in the right direction.
~ John C. Cosby

Support and encouragement help you stay on the trail. Seek out trusted encouragers who support your efforts. Be selective of your inner circle as they will determine your future.

1. Recruit your friends and family members to cheer you on toward your summit.
2. Invest in a coach or a mentor to hold you accountable along the way and keep you on course.
3. Remove the pride or stubbornness that holds you back from asking for help.
4. Find a support group surrounded by like-experienced and like-minded people where you can share your emotions without fear of judgment or rejection.

Ask and You Will Receive

Get over the notion that asking for help is a sign of weakness. People want to help, especially when they see you working toward a goal.

- Ask for help from people who want to see you grow.
- Seek out people who have respected ideas; who have the answers and will contribute to your success.
- Be accepting and thankful for others' help knowing that it is intended for your best interest.

You will be amazed with what transpires when you are comfortable and open to receiving help from others.

- A new relationship forms.
- A win-win encounter has taken place: the "helper" is pleased to help so you both have gained in the process.

Step 7
Choose Your Thoughts

Change the way you look at things, and the things you look at change.
~ Wayne Dyer

1. Speak words of affirmation, including words with power, conviction, and faith. "I WILL get through this", "I WILL reach my goal," I WILL overcome," "this too WILL pass," "I WILL not stop."
2. Train your brain to speak only positive, uplifting and forward-thinking thoughts about yourself: "I am strong," "I am a big deal," "I am good," "I am beautiful," "I am intelligent," "I am honest," "I am super woman or man," "I am loved."
3. Develop an undying enthusiasm for your goal pursuit. If you believe and buy into your WHY, your enthusiasm will naturally erupt.

Anticipate Positive Results

Take the high road in your thoughts. The following are points that will enhance your high road thinking and produce the psychological and emotional energy to enliven the drive.

- Engage in physical exercise that will release endorphins that contribute to a more consistent and positive attitude.
- Expect positive results.
- Choose to eat healthy and get proper sleep. These behaviors will dramatically improve how you see yourself and the world around you.
- Keep it fun. Fun has the power to engage your motivation and lighten the load that is before you.

Step 8
Step into the Arena

It is not the critic who counts; not the man who points out how the strong man stumbles, or where the doer or deeds could have done better. The credit belongs to the man who is actually in the arena, whose face is marred by dust and sweat and blood; who strives valiantly; who errs, who comes short again and again, because there is no effort without error and shortcoming; but who does actually strive to do the deeds; who knows great enthusiasms, the great devotions; who spends himself in a worthy cause; who at the best knows in the end the triumph of high achievement, and who at the worst, if he fails, at least fails while daring greatly, so that his place shall never be with those cold and timid souls who neither
know victory nor defeat.
~ President Theodore Roosevelt (1910)

1. Expect hard work and challenge. Grit your teeth and make the guttural sound that will push you to the next level.
2. Step out of your comfort zone and into the *Arena*. Get comfortable with being uncomfortable.

If you Fall, Get Back Up

As President Roosevelt articulated, the person who steps into the Arena and who is willing to endure failure, pain, and hardship will know real achievement as he or she advances toward his or her goal.

- Don't let disappointment and discouragement reverse your vision, but rather ignite the motivation to move you forward.
- There is no shame in falling. Falling only means failure when you don't get back up.
- Be willing to take risks. Risks carry the unknown element that will help you develop the insight, judgment and wisdom necessary for future decisions and actions.

Step 9
Faith in The Midst

*Your faith can move mountains
and your doubt can create them.*
~ Anonymous

Faith is a quiet strength and conviction of things unseen and unknown. *Faith in the future will give power to the present.* Faith gives you the mental and emotional capacity that breeds stability and security for you to press on.

1. Practice your faith by doing things that calm and settle your spirit. Go to church, spend time in nature, listen to uplifting music or a podcast, or attend an inspiring performance.
2. Feed your faith by starting your day in quiet. Listen, pay attention, read a devotion, write in a journal and release positive energy to lighten your way.
3. Seek out books or speakers that kindle the fuel that ignites your faith.
4. **Faith** voluntarily develops through action. Taking steps toward your summit or dream strengthens your faith.

Practice Faith

Exercise your faith by "stepping out" and "letting go" of things that you can't control. Stretch yourself to rely more on your spiritual center, for guidance and wisdom.

- Ask God or your spiritual guide for strength and courage to reach your summit.
- Meditate: Have moments of quiet where you can breathe slowly and quietly, allowing you to rest your mind and only welcome in positive and peaceful thoughts.
- Eliminate the "shiny object syndrome" so you can pay attention to where your spirit is guiding you.

As it has been paraphrased from the Bible, having faith as small as a mustard seed can move mountains and transform your life beyond your expectations.

- Believe, Trust and have Faith.
- Amazing things will happen.

Step 10
Put One Foot in Front of The Other

I never worry about action, but only inaction.
~ Winston Churchill

Action is a verb indicating movement. Once your previous steps are in place and your path appears clear, put your WHY, vision, plan, preparation, attitude, and initiative into Action.

1. Action and movement get the blood traveling and the heart beating faster, creating the enthusiasm for your goal.
2. Movement releases endorphins (the happy hormone) that provides you focus and energy.
3. Consider your pace. You may miss something along the way if you move too fast. On the other hand, if you move too slow, you may compromise the vitality needed to keep the bounce in your step.
4. Stop and smell the roses. This allows you to look around, identify landmarks along the way IF you get side tracked. Seeing the familiar will help you find your way back to the trail and onward to your goal.

Short to the Eye and Long to the Feet

The length of step, and the number of steps it takes for you to get to your goal or dream is uniquely different than anyone else. As you approach the pinnacle of your goal, you may find it is steeper, requiring you to take shorter steps and more steps to get to the end. The greatest challenges are often found closest to your summit.

As the crow flies, your summit may appear close, but your steps are many.

- DON'T STOP. Keep your eye on the prize.
- Remind yourself that each and every step taken toward your goal amounts to fewer and fewer steps to reach your dream.
- Your ACTIONS speak volumes. They can take you places you've always wanted to go with amazing views.

Step 11
Pull Out Your Compass

If you persevere, stick with it, work at it, you have a real opportunity to achieve. If you do your best and keep a true compass, you'll get there.
~ Edward Kennedy

There will be times that your designed route is not unfolding like you had planned. You may run into obstacles, a surprise storm, or an unexpected interruption. This is the natural course of things to anticipate. Don't be discouraged.

1. Your inner compass does not lie! Don't let interruptions make you second guess the worth of your dream.
2. If there is a will, there is a way. Your compass is your inner spirit that is designed to pester you until you have achieved your potential.
3. Keep the faith and believe you WILL get to the top.

Check your Map

Where your compass provides the inner knowing or divine beat to your dream, the map provides the big picture. Pulling out your map will indicate where you currently are and the route you are on. Your summit has not moved, but you may need to reroute your direction to get there. A tree is down across the trail, the river is far too wild and high to cross, or the trail has been washed away by a recent flood.

- Be creative and inspired to develop another way to get to your goal.
- The potential obstacles along the way are not signs or indicators to quit. Just don't stop.
- Eliminate self-sabotaging: Those defeating beliefs are danger signs for your progress.
- If your map blows away, know that your compass is perfectly designed to get you to your goal. You will find the way.

Step 12
Keep the Momentum

Everything worthwhile is uphill.
~ John Maxwell

A hiker gains energy after a rest break but if the break is too long, the muscles tighten making it harder to get up and go again. A mountain biker's best friend is momentum. If you slow or stop pedaling as you ride over roots and rocks, you and your bike will end up on the ground.

1. Keep putting one foot in front of the other, even if it is a small step.
2. Be intentional. Know that the journey ahead is uphill and you will get to the top.
3. Be deliberate. Eliminate the interruptions that pull you away from your summit.
4. Be consistent. Consistency moves you beyond mediocrity.
5. Be willful. Your will has amazing strength and will take you places you had no idea you would be.

Momentum is Not Speed

A consistent and steady hiker who takes fewer rest breaks gets to the next campsite at the same time as a fast hiker who takes many short breaks.

- Refrain from comparing your gain or progress to anyone else.
- A runner who signs up for a running event will always get a medal, regardless of the time it took her/him to complete the run. Run your race knowing you WILL cross the finish line.
- The WIN is in the commitment: Don't cheat yourself by taking a short cut or racing against someone else.

Step 13
Celebrate Your Summit

*When I have reached a summit, I leave it with
great reluctance, unless is it to reach
for another, higher one.*
~ Gustav Mahler

You made it! You accomplished more than you thought possible. Celebrations can be a gregarious invitation to others to celebrate with you or it can be a time to quietly revel alone in your achievement.

1. Take the time necessary to recognize your triumph and effort.
2. Celebrate your summit with gusto – fully honor your abilities and capabilities.
3. Be sure to recognize those friends and family members who gave you the encouragement and support in your journey.
4. Stand tall, with authentic gratitude to all those factors that had a hand in your success.

Don't Stay Long at the Top

In climbing a mountain, a climber does not stay long at the top. Inclement weather can develop, making the top an unsafe or dangerous place.

- Celebrating your success longer than necessary can create unhealthy pride, undermining the initial WHY of your goal.
- Staying in a state of euphoria at the top, can deter you from starting your next goal or summit.
- Ensure you have the strength, judgment and wisdom to return to your center in order to continue creating and pursuing future summits.

Step 14
Power of Reflection

You can't have a meaningful life without having self-reflection.
~ Oprah Winfrey

I have asked college students to write a reflection paper about a trip they had just experienced. Once, I had a student say, "I don't know how to reflect." Reflection is the process of rewinding the memory of your experience and making sense of what happened.

1. Was your WHY with you throughout the process?
2. What part of the process was the most difficult?
3. Where did you find your greatest strength?
4. Were there times throughout the process where you wanted to quit? Did you hear yourself saying "What is the point of this?"

Reflections to Take with You to the Next Summit

Reflective thoughts have the power to help you make sense of what happened as well as provide you the insight necessary in preparation for your next goal.

- Where and when did you find your greatest strength?
- What thoughts or interruptions were the enemy to your momentum? What would you do to prevent those enemies from showing up in the future?
- What was the consistent factor that kept you moving forward?

Answering these questions will give you the wisdom to step into the next goal more prepared and with resiliency.

- Learn from the best…yourself!

Step 15
Seek Your Next Summit

The summit is what drives us, yet the climb is what matters.
~ Conrad Anker

Reaching one summit is no excuse for stopping there. As you shine in your success and the view, remember that you have to return to the base of the mountain to plan and prepare for your next goal. Reaching one goal ignites your motivation to seek the next one.

1. Begin the process again by starting with WHY and follow the steps.
2. Change your plans or preparation steps, especially if it contributes to a smoother process in the end.
3. Capitalize on your previous experiences as they become your wisdom and judgment for the future.

Do it Again

If you haven't quite reached your summit, or you recognize there were elements that were missing along the way, take the opportunity to reroute your direction. Give it another push until you are pleased, satisfied and have reached your identified summit. There is no harm in returning to the same mountain over and over again. To not reach your goal can be as much of a motivator as reaching your goal.

- Value your journey and the climb.
- Know that your goal will not go away – it's not always about reaching the top.
- Be sensitive to timing and opportunity. Seize the moment when the moment is right for you.
- DO your best and BE your best. That is a summit in itself!

You've finished. Before you go...

Tweet/share that you finished this book.

Please star rate this book.

Reviews are solid gold to writers. Please take a few minutes to give us some itty bitty feedback.

ABOUT THE AUTHOR

Rená Koesler has spent her life observing and learning about what motivates others. She has earned her appreciation and understanding of others through attending personal growth and leadership development trainings but also in climbing mountains. Koesler desires to carve out opportunities for others in order to move them from stagnation to their ultimate potential.

In October 2019, she climbed Island Peak (20, 285 ft.) in Nepal, a peak she had yearned to climb for twenty years. This peak and the many before this one, revitalized and confirmed how purpose, preparation, focus, and will are critical in reaching your dream, goal, or summit.

Koesler is a Business Coach and Motivational Speaker. She works with business, educational and adventure audiences to initiate personal and professional growth in order to move toward one's potential. Reach out to her for consultation or speaking at:

http://www.RenaKoesler.com

I want to thank my father, who often said in my growing up years, *You can do anything you put your mind to.* I also want to recognize my brother, Gary, who inspired me to *Keep a song in my heart.*

If you enjoyed this Itty Bitty® book you might also like…

- **Your Amazing Itty Bitty® Self-Esteem Book** ~ By Jade Elizabeth

- **Your Amazing Itty Bitty® Purpose Book** ~ Gretchen Downey

- **Your Amazing Itty Bitty® Fear-Busting Book** ~ Lucetta Zaytoun

Or any of the many Amazing Itty Bitty® books available on line at www.ittybittypublishing.com

www.ingramcontent.com/pod-product-compliance
Lightning Source LLC
Chambersburg PA
CBHW052127110526
44592CB00013B/1786